Digital Success:

Mastering Online Advertising for Start-ups"

By

Maya Freya Woods

Copyright ©2024

DEDICATION

"I dedicate this book to God Almighty, who has been my guiding light throughout this journey.

ACKNOWLEDGEMENT

I thank my loving family, especially my mother whose unwavering support and understanding made this book possible. You are my inspiration and my rock.

Disclaimer

This book was written for informational purposes only. Every effort has been made to make this book as complete and accurate as possible. However, typographical or content errors may occur. Also, this book only provides information up to the date of publication. Therefore, this book should be used as a guide - not as a definitive resource. The purpose of this ebook is to educate. Neither the author nor the publisher warrant that the information contained in this book is completely complete and are not responsible for any errors or omissions. Neither the author nor the publisher shall have any responsibility or liability to any person or entity in respect of any loss or damage caused or alleged to be caused directly or indirectly by the book.

Harnessing the Digital Landscape for

Start-up Growth"

TABLE OF CONTENTS :

INTRODUCTION:...

Chapter 1 – How to Choose a Niche to Target :

What is a Niche and Why Does it
Matter?...

Why You Should Get More Specific When Choosing_
Your Niche..

The Power of Creating Your Own Niche............

Sites That Don't Fit Nicely Into Boxes...................

Combining Different Concepts: ....

Going More Niche ....

Trailblazing ....

Chapter 2: How to Choose a Business Name, Register a Domain, And Web hosting

Choosing Your Domain Name and Site Name ....

Branding...

Memorability ....

Uniqueness...

Other considerations ....

Buying Hosting & A Domain name ....

Get Started With The Most Basic Promotion...........

Chapter 3: Email Marketing

What Is Email Marketing?..

3-2:Using Email Marketing...................................

How To Get Your Email To Stand Out.....................

Receptivity..

Images & Clickability ....

Chapter 4: How To Get Traffic Through Paid
Advertising

The Good Of PPC Marketing ....

Designing Your Ad Accordingly................................

Targeting..

Chapter 5: How To Integrate Social Media To Grow Your Business:

Social Media Marketing Explained.... ....

Chapter 6: How To Start Monetizing.....................

Monetization Methods For Your Websites....................

Ad Networking...

Affiliation Products....................................

Your Own Products & Services...............................

Creating & Selling An Ebook ....

Chapter 7: Growth Hacks & Advanced Strategics To Skyrocket Your Business

Grow Hacks...

Guest
Posts...

Use Trending Hashtags
....

Influencer
Marketing..

Create Link
Bait..

Advanced
Strategies..

Conclusion
....

Introduction:

So you want to get started with internet marketing? As an internet marketer, you will be able to make money from the comfort of your own home with no limits on how far you can scale and grow your business.

It's very rewarding and it's a skill you can use to get jobs or sell to other companies. In short, you have made a very good decision! Maybe you've seen friends or people online who seem to be making money from the comfort of their own home - and they're actually doing great.

Now it's time to try it yourself! There's just one problem: it's all pretty complicated. If you are new to the internet marketing world, you might even be wondering how it is even possible to make money online without selling anything physical! Everyone seems to be promoting each other and no one is actually sending any physical products.

Then there's all the jargon: PPC, affiliate marketing, display ads, SEO, SMO, CTR, CPA... It's all a bit daunting and it's definitely not clear how and where to start. Then read on and we'll look at everything you need to know to become an internet marketing master and start making lots of money online.

CHAPTER ONE:
HOW TO CHOOSE NICHE
TO
TARGET

The first step to creating an online business is to choose what kind of online business you want to create. It starts with choosing a niche – what is the topic you will cover? In this chapter, you'll learn how to do this and see how this initial decision affects each subsequent step.

- What is a gap and why does it matter?

Every website should have a niche that describes the kind of things you will write about and the people you will write it for. Your site can be a "general" site or a personal blog that isn't about any particular topic, but there will at least be a "theme" or feeling that ties them together. You can write about books, coffee and the city, but that's still a niche and attracts a very specific type of people.

And knowing and understanding your niche is incredibly important if you hope to be able to make your website a success. Unfortunately, too many webmasters don't really fully understand their niche and their sites tend to suffer as a result.

Basically, you should know what your place is. For most site owners or bloggers, this will be an incredibly easy question to answer: the site will probably be about "soccer" or "technology", and that's fairly easy to define. However, if your site is more general, make a list of all the topics you regularly write about and then think about:

a) what ties them together and

b) what type of people will read them.

You've probably created a new niche, but if your future content meets the same criteria, you'll be on the money. The niche you choose should be primarily determined by your own interests. If you're going to live and breathe your blog for the next 10 years, then it HAS to be something you want to learn and write about. What's more, you won't be able to provide truly unique and valuable content if you don't know anything about the topic! And hiring professional writers does not guarantee that you will find someone who has a real passion and interest for the topic. While this is true, you also need to consider the viability of niche selection.

How competitive is it? Do you stand a chance against the biggest sites? How is it profitable and monetizable? We'll get into this more in later chapters, but the topic you choose should be something that people are willing to spend money on and that has a lot of opportunity for information products. Finance is the best field in this regard because there is so much money to be made in this subject. But you'll also find that you can make a lot of money writing about dating, fitness, or other topics that speak to a basic human need in this way.

- Why You Should Be More Specific When Choosing Your Niche:

To really succeed—and gain an edge over the competition—you need to dig a little deeper. Sure, your site may be a technology site, but what technology are you writing about? Who are you writing for? And what is the purpose of your website? For example, you can write about all kinds of technology, but you'll find yourself sticking more to the technology that's just around the corner.

Maybe you write a lot of big previews of upcoming technology. And maybe you write in a very technical way that is clearly aimed at people who know their stuff? This is a very different niche from a site that reviews basic commercial technology in a style that can appeal to the average customer. Again, you will have created your own niche, which should be completely unique.

You might put a football site on the safe side, but is it a dry site that deals with in-depth football coverage for true fanatics? Or is it more of a gossip site that is aimed at the typical "guy"? Again, these are slightly different niches and it's important to recognize the difference. If you can be consistent with your exact niche, you will find that your website offers something that not every other website does. You will have a specific audience and people who particularly like the way you approach the topic. Stick to your guns and it can make your website highly successful.

- The Power of Creating Your Own Niche :

This means that there are few niches left that a large number of people are interested in, but which are still not overcrowded in the market. This is especially difficult when you consider how important it is that you are genuinely interested in and know something about the niche you will be dealing with so regularly from now on. So how do you stand out without limiting your appeal or writing about something boring? One solution is to come up with your own niche and create a website that will be unlike any other. Here we look at how you can potentially achieve this.

- Sites That Don't Fit Nicely into Boxes

When you browse the web for inspiration on niches for your website, you will often find lists of categories such as 'fitness', 'making money', 'football', 'film' and others like these. Not every site though has to fit neatly into a category like this - it is possible to come up with a completely unique angle and to create a niche that wasn't there before. Take http://www.lifehacker.com for instance and http://www.lifehack.org. These sites exist in the same niche but go back a decade and that niche wouldn't have existed. These sites tie together lots of themes using a 'way of life' or 'attitude' to gel it all together. In this case that attitude is the 'hacker' attitude - where DIY applies to everything from self- improvement to making money; but you could just as easily build a site around any other central idea like.

- Combining Different Concepts:

 If you can't find a new topic to link items on your site, then another option is to simply combine several existing niches that you think will go well together. This way you will have your built-in audience - because you will get visitors from both of these existing niches - but at the same time you will have your own unique USP and be able to offer something that is different from everything else. Examples might include "bodybuilding and self-improvement", "making money online and city life", "travel and art" or "cafes, coffee and books". Alternatively, just taking a broader approach to your stories can help give your site more meat and put your niche more in context with other topics.

This strategy is also effective because it creates a number of simple marketing options that you can use to reach new audiences. For example, if you have a bodybuilding and self-improvement website, you will be able to promote your site on self-improvement forums without directly competing with those sites.

- Go more niche:

As opposed to expanding your niche, another option is to be even more specific by finding a category within a category. Again, this will allow you to market to sites that would otherwise see you as competition, and help make SEO easier by targeting your target. An example might be targeting a certain type of movie, such as 80s action movies, a specific era of music, or perhaps a specific type of exercise, such as bodyweight training itself.

- Trailblazing :

Finally If you have the means, you might even consider creating a niche before you build your website. For example, if you run a software company and release new software or a new computer game, you'll likely find that it generates interest and fans.

By creating a website dedicated to the software you've released, you can provide an official website for that interest and create an almost symbiotic relationship between your software and your website, where the success of one helps the success of the other.

This works for any kind of product and service that captures the public's attention. Although not every webmaster will have a product to promote, it is important for businesses and entrepreneurs not to miss this opportunity when it presents itself.

Chapter 2

How to Choose a Business Name, Register a Domain, And Web Hosting:

Now you have your place, it's time to turn this basic theme into a business model. This is where it can get complicated for some, but it's also the most fun and exciting part! And it all starts with choosing your business name, which will most likely also be your website name, which will most likely also be your domain name (the address that visitors type into their browser to find your website.

- Choosing your domain name and Site name :

If you're getting ready to launch a new website, there are a few things you'll need to do in preparation before you even start thinking about content writing or SEO. Of course, one of the most essential starting points is finding a hosting service and choosing a domain name for your website or blog. This will give you a place to store the files that make up your website and for your visitors to access them. But deciding on a domain name is more than just a practical matter, it will also have a huge impact on the way your visitors view your site and on the way to promoting it. Here we look at how to choose a domain name that makes sense from both a business and creative perspective.

- Branding :

Coming up with a name for your website that you can build a brand around makes sense for several reasons. First, Google has explicitly stated that it will try to give more importance to tags and bury "exactly named domains" (keyword URLs) in an effort to show higher quality sites. But at the same time, if you can create a brand name, it gives you more opportunities for future expansion, meaning you can more easily promote your site and create awareness while using the same brand in your advertising.

- Memorability :

Of course, if you want people to visit your site often and spread the word, then it makes sense to choose a URL that is easy to remember. If your website title is too long or nonsensical, it will mean that people will want to come back to your website or tell others about it. Avoid complex combinations of dashes and underscores and try to make the URL as clever as possible.

- Uniqueness :

Even though Google no longer gives any advantage to exact name domains, typing your URL into Google is still one of the ways people are likely to get to your website. But if your URL isn't unique at all, you'll be buried somewhere around page 100. In that regard, branding the company "Apple" would be a bad move (luckily, Apple already had a lot of influence behind them). Likewise, a unique company name will help you to be more memorable again and also help you avoid using any trademarked names. Of course, you may also want to do some research to make sure the name you want is available and that you are legally allowed to use it. A unique domain will also allow you to purchase similar domains (for typos, etc.) with less chance of them already being taken.

- Other Considerations:

In addition to these points, there are many more aspects to keep in mind, although the degree to which they apply to your website will vary. For example, if your business is likely to be listed in alphabetical order, coming up with a URL starting with "A" or even "1" might be a good way to get to the top. Likewise, you may want to consider the length of your domain, and of course it's all just academic until you factor in price and availability...

Top Tip: While you don't necessarily need to trademark your domain name, it's a good idea to make sure that no one has already bought it. Check that there are no websites with very similar names, and also do a trademark search to make sure yours

is unique
(https://www.uspto.gov/trademark).

- Buying hosting and a domain name :

Now that you have a name for your website, the next step is to create it. This means doing several things,

Investing in web hosting
Buying your domain name
Creating the basic foundation of your website.

Web hosting is where your site will be stored. Popular options include:

➤ Bluehost – www.bluehost.com

➤ GoDaddy – www.godaddy.com

➤ HostGator – www.hostgator.com

All of these will provide what you need to get started, although our recommendation is to choose BlueHost. Web hosting basically gives you space on a huge, constantly connected computer called a server. You upload the files that make up your website to that computer, and then when someone types your URL into the address bar, they'll see those files.

This is why, of course, you also need to buy a domain name. You can do this separately, but the good news is that most web hosts will also allow you to buy a domain name directly through their site. Once you click that you want to register, this will be the first thing you do before you pay for the store.

There are a lot of different options and settings when choosing a plan for your hosting. When you're starting out as an internet marketer, you won't have a lot of traffic to begin with, nor will you have to deal with a lot of very large files - so the most basic options will do. Finally, you need to set up the basics of your website.

My term and I highly recommend using WordPress for this. WordPress is a completely free tool that is easily available on most hosting plans and can be installed from your dashboard with a single click. This then gives you a basic website and allows you to easily add new posts, change a number of settings and even install brand new themes and mini apps.

WordPress powers more than a quarter of all websites on the Internet, is used by many of the world's best-known brands, and is completely open-source and fully customizable. There is a huge support community (just do a quick search for "how to set up a WordPress website" to get started) and it works with the largest share of third-party apps and plugins. In short, there is no reason not to use WordPress.

- Get Started with the Most Basic Promotion:

In the next few chapters, we'll look at some advanced marketing and promotion tools you can use to get your website over the top. This includes social media marketing, email marketing and more. But before we get ahead of ourselves, you might just want to start populating your site to get more traffic. Your job now is to find the blog section of your website and add a new post that is directly related to your niche, once a week to once a day (the more the better).

Just adding more content to your site gives visitors a reason to keep checking back, sharing your content, and considering buying whatever you're selling. Likewise, adding content will help give Google something it can use to identify the topic of your site, helping it present your page when people search for relevant terms. Keep in mind that you can do this much more effectively if you also use basic SEO. This means integrating search terms. This is a more advanced form of marketing, but one you can look at as you progress.

- Chapter 3 – Email Marketing:

So now you have your website and some content, it's time to start actively promoting it - start getting people to go there. How are you doing it? One of the most effective options is email marketing, and that's where we'll start. • What is email marketing? While social media has come and gone and SEO (that's search engine optimization) has gone through many changes that have led people to question its reliability and effectiveness, email marketing is something that has been around for the longest time and has been proven not. signs to go anywhere. Most of us still start our days by checking email, and any messages we find there are still likely to be read and noticed. To get started with email marketing, you first need to get something called an autoresponder. This is a tool that you use to collect email addresses and then send out multiple messages at a set time. While you might think this is something you can do without a mailing list, that's absolutely not true. To successfully collect and manage emails, you'll need to deal with spam and make sure people actually want to be on your list - both of which will require the use of a confirmation email. You'll also need to handle unsubscribing people, you'll want to maintain "list hygiene" by deleting stale emails, and you'll want to be able to track who's opening your emails and which ones are the most successful. None of this could be done manually. Consider one of the following autoresponders and choose the most basic plan: MailChimp

www.mailchimp.com

GetResponse

www.getresponse.com

AWeber

www.aweber.com

Other good options include: ConvertKit, Drip, and ActiveCampaign. With this tool, you will be able to create a form to collect user data.

You can then add this to your website in the sidebar or at the bottom of each post.

WordPress allows you to do this easily with plugins.

- Using Email Marketing :

Collecting emails when someone lands on your website is an effective and useful strategy for converting visitors into leads. Now you can offer them new products and encourage them to come back to your website.

One way to leverage your email marketing is to send emails that provide additional content – just like your blog posts. Another option is to send an email to people talking about all the posts you've recently made on your site to encourage them to visit again. Then, when you have a product to sell, send a message to promote that product and increase sales. This will be discussed in the next chapter. The thing is, when you use email marketing, you don't rely on your visitors to check your website every day. Now you have a way to reach them—and it's a way that doesn't depend on a third-party site like Google or Facebook.

- How to Make Your Emails Stand Out

While email marketing has remained effective, it has changed quite a bit over the past decade – even if it might not be obvious at first glance. The biggest change, of course, is the way we check our emails. For most of us, this is now done on the go and constantly through our smartphones and tablets. Instead of getting home and checking 20 emails at once, we instead receive emails throughout the day as we go about our work. This in turn means that each email is more likely to 'stand out' from the others and be noticed on its own merits, but it also means that we've become accustomed to just brushing them off as annoying. If you want your email marketing campaign to be successful, you need to take this into account and factor it into the way you design your subject headings and how you send your messages.

- Receptivity:

When you're creating your mailing list, you'll obviously need to choose the names on it based on who you think will be receptive to your message. It should be a targeted mailing list so that the people you contact find your product or service relevant - it's no good sending a children's clothing catalogue to Priest. At the same time, however, you need to think about the time when your mailing list will be most receptive to your message.

This means both in terms of the point they are in their life (children's clothing catalogues will be more effective to send to people in their 30s) and the time of day. What time do they get home from work? When are they likely to be sitting down to answer emails and when is their inbox more likely to be empty?

Sending materials on a Sunday morning will be much more effective than sending them at 3pm on a Monday – so get as much information as possible about your recipients and consider the time factor in your marketing. Oh, and if you can get your mailing list to agree with your marketing information, you'll find that they're always much more receptive to what you have to say.

- Images and Clickability:

If you want to get your recipients to buy something or visit your website, you need to think about the images you use in your message. Using a clickable button instead of a small hyperlink will always improve your click-through rate because it will be more attractive to click. Similarly, using images can help make a quick visual impression on visitors.

But then you have to consider the fact that many email accounts will block images from unknown senders and that downloading large images may bother people. Keep your messages relatively simple and use images sparingly for more impact. Due to the wide range of devices your message will be seen on, it helps you avoid limiting your impact.

- Chapter 4 - How to Get Traffic Through Paid Advertising :

PPC stands for Pay Per Click and refers to the use of advertising networks such as Facebook Ads or AdWords to promote your website or product. Basically, with any of these services, you agree to pay a set amount for each click on your ad, so you can avoid spending money on a failed campaign. Still, you have to think about how you're going to turn the traffic you get into profit, and you have to think about how to get the right people to click on your ads. There are a number of tricks to make a successful and especially profitable PPC campaign, so here we will see what they are.

- The Goal of PPC Marketing:

This is really the most important thing to keep in mind; that the PPC campaign that gets the most clicks isn't necessarily the most successful because that means you'll actually spend the most money. You only want people to click on your ads if they're likely to make you money once they come to your site—if they're likely to be returning visitors who click your ads, for example, or if they're likely to buy products that you are selling. One of the best ways to leverage your PPC campaign is to link directly to the landing page where you sell the product. Then if you can get the product to sell for say $30 an hour, then you can afford to pay $1 per click if you sell at least 1/3 of the visitors (this is called the conversion rate). This way you still make a profit. PPC ads are displayed based on a bidding system in fractions of seconds. This means that the more you decide to pay per "per click" (you can set this amount), the more your ad will appear in relevant places. By increasing the conversion rate on your website and improving your ads, you can spend more money and get your ad in front of more people – increasing your profits. In order to work with this, you need to focus much more on the CTR (Click Through Rate) on your page and the quality of traffic that PPC advertising brings you. If you trick people into clicking on your ad and then they only spend a minute on your page, then you're really just wasting money. Likewise, if your site doesn't do a good enough job of convincing people to buy, then again, you're effectively wasting money.

- Design your ad accordingly:

As such, you should aim to create an ad that will get the attention you want from the right people, and only if they are likely to buy. In other words, then you can consider including a price in your ad, the reason being that it will allow you to drive away people who are not willing to spend that kind of money - which is only good, because you don't want to pay for them to come to your website. However, the important thing is that your ad is so eye-catching However, it is still important that your ad catches the attention of the people you want to see. Be professional, honest and sincere, and then if you focus on the CTR of your landing page, you can generate money very reliably that way.

- Targeting:

Whether you choose to use Facebook Ads or Google AdWords, one of the most important aspects of an effective campaign is targeting. In other words, your emails are reaching the right people – people who are likely to buy from you. Again, this increases conversion, which means you can spend more money, which means you increase your profits. AdWords displays ads on Google search engines based on what people are searching for.

You choose the search terms you want to target, and when someone searches for that phrase, your ad will appear at the top as a "sponsored result." Facebook Ads displays ads on a user's home feed on Facebook based on their interests, demographics, and other data. That way, you can choose to only show your fitness book to people who are interested in working out (but could also list their weight as slightly heavier!). Which option is better for you? This depends on the nature of your monetization (which we'll talk more about in a moment).

However, keep in mind that while Facebook allows you to target audiences based on more information, Google allows you to target people based on their intent. In other words, if someone searches for "buy a fitness ebook", then it's telling you that they actually want to buy an ebook. So it might be easier to convert them. If you're still trying to make money from ads (and we'll discuss this option again soon), you may not be able to put as much money into your business plan.

- Chapter 5 – How to Integrate Social Media to Grow Your Business:

Now you have PPC and email marketing that is used to drive traffic to your website and increase sales of the product (which we haven't added yet). But you still have more tools at your disposal for even more custom driving. One such tool is social networks. Social media is an extremely useful resource when it comes to getting traffic because it basically allows you to talk to your audience as a human being.

We all use social media so we understand how it works. This is definitely NOT necessarily true about Google! Social media is also powerful because it allows you to build relationships with your audience.

This in turn can be extremely powerful in getting people to become loyal to your site, sign up for your emails and get them to visit your site directly – Google or not! • Social Media Marketing Explained Sometimes it can feel a bit like guesswork when trying to build a following on social media – especially when you're just starting out. At first, you'll feel like every post you write is falling on fertile ground, and after spending ages coming up with interesting things to say, you'll be met with the sound of silence in return.

And what kind of content should you even be targeting? And how do you get people to listen?

While it may seem like you're just groping blindly in the dark, there is a proven method to finding success on social media, and it's perfectly possible to systematise the process to ensure rapid success. Here we look at how to implement the best strategy and use the right tools to start generating followers and take the guesswork out of social media marketing.

- The Strategy:

The process of building a successful social media campaign is fairly simple when you

know how. The goal is to continually
bring value to your audience through
informative and interesting posts that you
regularly upload to your various accounts.
But at the same time, you need to make
sure you have a strong brand identity
between these accounts. This means you
should have the same account name, logo,
and images on Facebook and Tumblr as
you do on Twitter and Instagram. You
should create multiple channels that your
visitors can use to find you and use them
all synergistically. This is where you should
start building your following. This is the
hardest part when starting out, as
followers beget followers – in other words,
people are more likely to sign up once they

see that other people have. To keep those followers coming, you should make sure you have social media buttons on your website or blog. This doesn't just mean share buttons – but links directly to your account that your visitors can follow to find you. Alternatively, you can use more sophisticated widgets to showcase your feeds, such as a Twitter feed (this will have the added bonus of making your website look more active). This is very important and even though you might not think it would work, just having those links there will be enough to get some visitors over there. You will continue to post from there. And you can use some of the following tools and strategies to start getting even more followers just like you... A few quick tips: • Use the most popular hashtags when posting • If you can't be on every social platform (which is ideal), then try being on ones that match your content creation style and that target the same audience as you.

• How to Grow Your Connections: Do you want to know one of the biggest motivations for people? A sense of duty. This means that if someone feels that you have done something for them, they will feel compelled to do something back until they feel that they have done so much for you. This powerful tip can be helpful in building your social media following.

Simply add people and they'll add you back. Or retweet their posts and they will retweet yours. It really is that easy. This means you don't want to waste your time adding millions of followers and then retweeting their stuff if you're not going to get any benefits out of it. This is where a tool like Social Rank can come in very handy – it tells you which of your followers you're most interested in, and which of them have the biggest following of their own. A very powerful thing if you want to know who to retweet and who to hang out with more generally! Social Rank also shows the importance of quality over quantity when it comes to your social media followers. In other words, it's better to have one influential and active follower than a million who don't care about you and have no real reach. Even better, you want to find the people you want to add who are potential customers - which is kind of like NeedTagger

(www.needtagger.com) comes in. This lets you find people who are likely to be interested in your products or services!

- How to Improve Your Posts :

As you post, you also need to ensure you are keeping track of how effective those posts are so that you know whether what you're doing is working.

LikeAlyzer (www.likealyzer.com) lets you see which of your Facebook posts are successful and what your competition is doing – as well as providing you with actionable tips for your own page. In general, make sure that your posts are using popular hashtags and that they're focused on hot topics.

BuzzSumo (www.buzzsumo.com) is a very useful tool that will enable you to easily see what topics are currently popular while you can see trending tags on Twitter itself.

Of course you can also use tools like Buffer (www.buffer.com) to save you time actually posting

- Do not give up!

Hopefully these tips have helped you feel more confident about your social media campaign. If you find you're not an overnight hit, don't worry—these things take time and a combination of trial and error, and lots of data will only help you refine your strategy. It's not an art, it's a science, and once you understand it, it's an incredibly powerful tool to use.

- Chapter 6 – How to Start
  Monetizing:

If you got into this with the goal of making money from your website... then what are you waiting for? If you have people actively visiting your website and reading your content, then there are many ways to generate a lot of profit from it without making major compromises and without affecting their experience.

You'll be making money while you sleep, and you'll find yourself getting richer without actually doing anything once you get it all set up. That's right, we're finally getting to that point. It's an internet marketer's dream! The only small obstacle between you and your happy passive income future is deciding which monetization method to use and deciding exactly how to turn your website into a cash cow.

Here we look at some of the options available to you and their strengths and weaknesses. And for the rest of you who already run successful websites that make money, this still applies to you – because you may not be making the most of your website in this regard and you can learn something.

• Ways to monetize your website:

Below are some of the most effective monetization methods for any website. Just keep in mind that you don't necessarily have to choose between them. Often the best strategy is to use them together!

- Ad networks:

Every webmaster knows about ad networks. The idea here is simply that you sign up as a publisher and then place a small snippet of code on your site. This code then automatically generates ads from participating advertisers based on the content on your site, which in turn ensures that the most relevant ads are displayed on your site and that you don't have to worry about chasing down advertisers yourself. After that, in most cases, you will be paid per click every time someone clicks on one of your ads.

The most obvious ad network that most people use is Google AdSense, which is known for relatively high payouts and is a reliable and easy-to-implement system. Some companies make a living from AdSense.

However, AdSense isn't the only ad network on the block, and there are some with slightly less stringent requirements (for all you gambling site owners out there) that are less likely to simply close your account (as several webmasters have reported that google does the same you can choose to combine multiple ad networks, you can do this with AdSense if you're using another similar network, but if the method is different enough you can double up if you want - for example you can use "text" ads like Kontera. However, Kontera has a relatively very low CPC (cost per click) and in some cases can distract from clicks from Google instead of doubling your clicks as you may have hoped. However, CTR does have some value for sites with very high traffic volumes.

- Affiliate Products :

Selling affiliate products is often more profitable based on the number of clicks, but you will have a much lower conversion rate because people have to actually put their money where their mouth is and buy something to get any benefit. Amazon has perhaps the most popular affiliate service that allows you to get a cut for recommending a number of their products. However, this is again a fairly low cut and you can get more by using more services. For example, most supplement stores have an affiliate program if you are a webmaster, and Clickbank gives you a great way to find many more affiliates and sell products like ebooks.

- Your Own Products and Services:

In all of these cases, without exception, you have to recognize that if you're making money this way, you're at the bottom of the heap. At the end of the day, you're getting paid to send people away from your website, and because these advertisers are willing to do that, it tells you that they're worth more than what you're getting paid for them.
The most effective way to earn from a visitor is to sell products and services. Now, you can do this by buying and

selling items wholesale and making a small profit on each, but this will require a lot of time, administration and storage space. It's better to make money by selling products and services that you can mass produce for free. The best example of this is selling ebooks and even printing books (where you use POD services) which require no work on your part once they are set up.

Likewise, you can sell subscriptions to your site, copywriting and web services, or even a "course" that can consist of several regular emails, a book, and a subscription in one package. And people will be willing to pay a lot for it if you sell it well. However, eBooks offer the easiest way to start making money from your website right away, so let's first look at how you can start making money this way.

- Creating and Selling an eBook First :

you need to create your product. It could be a book, course, video series, or any number of other things. The theme here is up to you, but self-improvement of any kind—like dating, losing weight, or making money—is often very important. Make sure you stand behind your product and believe strongly in it, as this will help you believe in your own marketing and push it wherever you can. If you are embarrassed or ashamed of your own product, you need to reconsider.

Another tip is to think about your target audience. Pick one market and design your product specifically for them and you will have more success than just vaguely targeting your product at everyone. Think about your demographic and create an imaginary person in your mind who would be your ideal customer. Then when designing your product, ask yourself – would the 'Crowd' like it?

- Filter Visitors :

Now you want to be able to direct your visitors as needed to convert them from visitors to money. Here's a quick question that can often be very revealing about your website - when someone first visits your home page, what is the first thing you want them to do? If you can't definitively answer that right now, you'll find that your visitors won't know where to go either.

That's what you should want from your visitors: an email address. A great way to do this is to give something away for free. By donating, for example, a free e-book chapter or a free video from your course, you will be able to exchange them for an email address. Once you have their address, you'll be able to offer them sales directly through their inbox. The great thing is that even if they don't stay on your site, you'll still be able to sell and promote them.

- Chapter 7 – Growth Hacks and Advanced Strategies to Skyrocket Your Business :

Now everything is in place. Now you have excellent website designed in WordPress, with a smart branding and domain name. You have a design that is born out of the niche you chose, you have regular content coming out, and all of that content is directing your visitors to either buy a product, click an ad, or sign up to your mailing list – you're making money either way.

But that's just the start. Now it's time to grow. And the good news is that there are some very quick and effective ways to do this. This chapter is going to share "growth hacks" and advanced strategies. However, it's not just going to share the usual slew.

Rather, it's going to contain the methods used by the biggest brands in the world, and the key difference between a highly successful website, and one that just turns over a little profit before going under.

Growth Hacks

Growth hacks are techniques you can use to get ahead of your website promotion. Basically, they allow you to bypass the usual gradual trajectory of a site's popularity and instead create a much steeper climb.

Here are some examples:

•Guest Posts :

A guest post is a post that you write and give to another content creator for free. The idea is that this post then links back to your site. They get free content but in return you get a link that will improve your Google ranking AND lead to many direct clicks from following these creators. Not only is it a link, but it will also act as a testimonial of sorts from someone these people trust!

•Use trending hashtags :

Especially when posting on social media, it makes a huge difference. If you're not sure what hashtags to use, check out the ones your top competitors are using. Likewise, creating content based on current trends can be an extremely beneficial strategy.

•Influencer Marketing:

Influencer marketing is a strategy that involves getting someone with a large following to mention your blog (often called a shout-out). It works very well because you can get clicks from say 10% of that person's audience. If they have 1 million followers, then that is a HUGE influx of traffic!

•Create Link Bait :

Link bait is the term for a post that is so useful and so great that you can almost guarantee that people will start linking to it for free, giving you free traffic and a better reputation in the eyes of Google. Good examples of link bait include posts that are complete guides to a topic, as well as those that argue a controversial point.

• Advanced Strategies:

Growth hacks may be popular, but it's more important to take your skills to the next level and develop serious, advanced strategies used by big brands and blogs. An example of this is SEO. SEO can be extremely effective in helping you get more visitors to your website, especially if you use SEO along with a lot of content with affiliate links. Some quick and effective tips for good SEO: • Use a tool like

Keywordtool.io to find search terms • Be careful with your keywords when writing - 1% density is more than enough.

• Use related terms and synonyms

• Include your keyword in the opening and closing paragraphs, one header and page title Another example of an advanced strategy is creating a YouTube channel.

This is one of the best ways to build a relationship with your visitors and gain more exposure. If you take the time to create a successful channel, it can be a game changer. And finally, make sure you put a lot of time and effort into the brand.

The key to a very successful brand is to make sure that when someone looks at your website or your logo, they know what they're talking about.

- Conclusion:

This book taught you the tools and skills you need to get started with internet marketing. It is more important to act. Creating your website is one of the most important things you can do to succeed online because you are building on your own platform. Use social channels combined with SEO and paid advertising to get an audience for your website and offers to build your brand and business. Above all, never stop learning. Those who are successful today started from the bottom.